This journal belongs to

....

$\mathcal{B}$y reading the Scriptures,

I am so renewed that all nature

seems renewed around me and with me.

The sky seems to be a pure, a cooler blue,

the trees a deeper green. The whole world

is charged with the glory of God,

and I feel fire and music under my feet.

THOMAS MERTON

The LORD is the everlasting God, the Creator of the ends of the earth....
He gives strength to the weary and increases the power of the weak....Those who hope
in the LORD will renew their strength. They will soar on wings like eagles;
they will run and not grow weary, they will walk and not be faint.

ISAIAH 40:28–29, 31 NIV

I love to think of nature as an unlimited broadcasting station through which God speaks to us every hour, if we will only tune in.

GEORGE WASHINGTON CARVER

The very same God who created the universe and all the marvels
in it also deliberately created you. You are a treasure to Him,
a masterpiece, a beloved child. Trust Him.

God dwells in His creation and is everywhere indivisibly present in all His works. He is transcendent above all His works even while He is immanent within them.

A. W. TOZER

No matter what storm you face, you need to know that God loves you.
He has not abandoned you.

FRANKLIN GRAHAM

The day is yours, and yours also the night; you established the sun and moon.

PSALM 74:16 NIV

Our Creator would never have made such lovely days and have given us the deep hearts to enjoy them…unless we were meant to be immortal.

NATHANIEL HAWTHORNE

We cannot always trace God's hand, but we can always trust God's heart.

CHARLES SPURGEON

The more I study nature, the more I stand amazed at the work of the Creator.

LOUIS PASTEUR

God made you so you could share in His creation, could love and laugh and know Him.

TED GRIFFEN

The heavens proclaim the glory of God. The skies display his craftsmanship.

PSALM 19:1 NLT

We...see God reaching out to us in every wind that blows, every sunrise and sunset, every cloud in the sky, every flower that blooms, and every leaf that fades.

OSWALD CHAMBERS

The grandeur of nature is only the beginning. Beyond the grandeur is God.

ABRAHAM JOSHUA HESCHE

The God who created, names, and numbers the stars in the heavens also numbers the hairs of my head.... What matters to me matters to Him, and that changes my life.

ELISABETH ELLIOT

You are a creation of God unequaled anywhere in the universe....
Thank Him for yourself and then for all the rest of His glorious handiwork.

NORMAN VINCENT PEALE

$\mathscr{L}$ook at the birds of the air; they do not sow or reap or store away in barns,
and yet your heavenly Father feeds them. Are you not much more valuable than they?

MATTHEW 6:26 NIV

Loving Creator, help me reawaken my childlike
sense of wonder at the delights of Your world!

MARILYN MORGAN HELLEBERG

To be thrilled by the stars at night; to be elated over a bird's nest
or a wildflower in spring—these are some of the rewards of the simple life.

JOHN BURROUGHS

*W*ho can hold an autumn leaf in their hand or sift the warm white sand
on the beach and not wonder at the Creator of it all?

WENDY MOORE

Stretch out your hand and receive the world's wide gift of joy, appreciation, and beauty.

CORINNE ROOSEVELT ROBINSON

You formed the mountains by your power…you quieted the raging oceans with their pounding waves…. Those who live at the ends of the earth stand in awe of your wonders. From where the sun rises to where it sets, you inspire shouts of joy.

PSALM 65:5–8 NLT

In our strength, this world is a daunting place, but we are not limited to our strength alone. Almighty God offers all that He is to us.

....
....
....
....
....
....
....
....
....
....
....
....
....
....
....
....
....
....
....
....
....
....
....
....
....

God created the universe, but He also created you. God knows you, God loves you, and God cares about the tiniest details of your life.

BRUCE BICKEL AND STAN JANTZ

Some days, it is enough encouragement just to watch the clouds break up and disappear, leaving behind a blue patch of sky and bright sunshine that is so warm upon my face. It's a glimpse of divinity; a kiss from heaven.

The finger of God was on me all day—nothing else could have saved me.

DUKE OF WELLINGTON

*Each day the LORD pours his unfailing love upon me,
and through each night I sing his songs, praying to God who gives me life.*

PSALM 42:8–9 NLT

Be refreshed today—renew your strength
by looking to the One who calls the stars by name,
who sees when a sparrow falls,
and who knows your every need.

In whatever direction you turn, you will see God coming to meet you; nothing is void of Him, He Himself fills all His work.

SENECA THE YOUNGER

You aren't an assembly-line product. You were deliberately planned, specifically gifted, and lovingly positioned on the earth by the Master Craftsman.

MAX LUCADO

*S*omething deep in all of us yearns for God's beauty,
and we can find it no matter where we are.

SUE MONK KIDD

I wait quietly before God, for my victory comes from him.

PSALM 62:1 NLT

*W*hat gives me the most hope every day is God's grace;
knowing that His grace is going to give me the strength for whatever I face,
knowing that nothing is a surprise to God.

RICK WARREN

*W*hat comes into our minds when we think about God
is the most important thing about us.

A. W. TOZER

God writes the gospel not in the Bible alone,
but also on trees and in the flowers and clouds and stars.

MARTIN LUTHER

In everyone's heart there is a secret nerve that answers to the vibrations of beauty.

CHRISTOPHER MORLEY

*S*earch high and low, scan skies and land, you'll find nothing
and no one quite like GOD...powerful and faithful from every angle.

PSALM 89:6–8 MSG

*E*arth's crammed with heaven,
And every common bush afire with God.

ELIZABETH BARRETT BROWNING

I can't change the direction of the wind,
but I can adjust my sails to always reach my destination.

JIMMY DEAN

If we are children of God, we have a tremendous treasure in nature and will realize that it is holy and sacred.

OSWALD CHAMBERS

The whole world is a love letter from God.

PETER KREEFT

As the deer longs for streams of water, so I long for you, O God.

PSALM 42:1 NLT

Nature is God's self-portrait. It is not God, since God transcends what He has created, but it reveals in physical form what He is like spiritually.

STEVE DeWITT

Keep your face to the sunshine and you cannot see a shadow.

HELEN KELLER

Keep close to nature's heart...break clear away once in a while and climb a mountain or spend a week in the woods. Wash your spirit clean.

JOHN MUIR

*L*ove beauty; it is the shadow of God on the universe.

GABRIELA MISTRAL

In his hand are the depths of the earth, and the mountain peaks belong to him.

PSALM 95:4 NIV

In the beginning, God created. He imagined the world into being. Every flower, animal, mountain, and rainbow is a product of God's creative imagination.

JILL M. RICHARDSON

*One who loves is borne on wings; he runs,
and is filled with joy; he is free and unrestricted.*

THOMAS à KEMPIS

One touch of nature makes the whole world kin.

SHAKESPEARE

The extent of the whole universe is but a point, an atom, compared to His immensity.

JEAN DE LA BRUYÈRE

He set the earth on its foundations; it can never be moved.

PSALM 104:5 NIV

God stepped out on space,
And He looked around and said,
"I'm lonely—I'll make Me a world."

JAMES WELDON JOHNSON

I have never been a millionaire. But I have enjoyed a crackling fire, a glorious sunset, a walk with a friend, and a hug from a child. There are plenty of life's tiny delights for all of us.

JACK ANTHONY

*S*how the wonder of your great love....
Keep me as the apple of your eye;
hide me in the shadow of your wings.

PSALM 17:7–8 NIV

*T*rust to God to weave your thread into the great web,
though the pattern shows it not yet.

GEORGE MACDONALD

How ow blessed all those in whom you live.... They wind through lonesome valleys, come upon brooks, discover cool springs and pools brimming with rain!

PSALM 84:5–6 MSG

To me a lush carpet of pine needles or spongy grass is more welcome
than the most luxurious Persian rug.

HELEN KELLER

In wilderness I sense the miracle of life,
and behind it our scientific accomplishments fade to trivia.

CHARLES LINDBERGH

Everybody needs beauty as well as bread, places to play in and pray in, where nature may heal and give strength to body and soul.

JOHN MUIR

Nothing in all creation is so like God as stillness.

MEISTER ECKHART

If I rise on the wings of the dawn, if I settle on the far side of the sea, even there your hand will guide me...[and] hold me fast.

PSALM 139:9–10 NIV

And this be our motto, "In God is our trust."

FRANCIS SCOTT KEY

God's love is literally infinite. It is the shoreless sea we are destined to swim in, surf in, and grow in forever.

PETER KREEFT

When the soul has laid down its faults at the feet of God, it feels as though it had wings.

EUGÉNIE DE GUÉRIN

God's love is like a river springing up...and flowing endlessly through His creation, filling all things with life and goodness and strength.

THOMAS MERTON

Your faithfulness extends to every generation, as enduring as the earth you created.

PSALM 119:90 NLT

The Christian is one whose imagination should fly beyond the stars.

FRANCIS A. SCHAEFFER

A God wise enough to create me and the world I live in is wise enough to watch out for me.

PHILIP YANCEY

....

....

....

....

....

....

....

....

....

....

....

....

....

....

....

....

....

....

....

....

....

....

....

....

....

*I*f God was faithful to you yesterday,
you have reason to trust Him for tomorrow.

WOODROW KROLL

God knows more about tomorrow than I can remember about today.

THOM DUMA

You will keep in perfect peace all who trust in you,
all whose thoughts are fixed on you!

ISAIAH 26:3 NLT

Nothing is more beautiful than the loveliness of the woods before sunrise.

GEORGE WASHINGTON CARVER

*S*tars may be seen from the bottom of a deep well, when they cannot be discerned from the top of a mountain. So are many things learned in adversity.

CHARLES SPURGEON

What can be more foolish than to think that all this rare fabric of heaven and earth could come by chance, when all the skill of art is not able to make an oyster!

JEREMY TAYLOR

The least movement is of importance to all nature.
The entire ocean is affected by a pebble.

BLAISE PASCAL

You care for people and animals alike, O Lord.
How precious is your unfailing love, O God!
All humanity finds shelter
in the shadow of your wings.

PSALM 36:6–7 NLT

God creates beauty so we can know what He is like....
Creation reflects this with seeable, tastable, touchable,
hearable, and smellable reflections of His glory and beauty.

STEVE DeWITT

*S*urely there is something in the unruffled calm of nature that overawes
our little anxieties and doubts: the sight of the deep-blue sky
and the clustering stars above seem to impart a quiet to the mind.

JONATHAN EDWARDS

....
....
....
....
....
....
....
....
....
....
....
....
....
....
....
....
....
....
....
....
....
....
....

Ellie Claire® Gift & Paper Expressions
Franklin, TN 37067
EllieClaire.com
Ellie Claire is a registered trademark of Worthy Media, Inc.

On Wings Like Eagles Journal
© 2017 by Ellie Claire
Published by Ellie Claire, an imprint of Worthy Publishing Group, a division of Worthy Media, Inc.

ISBN 978-1-63326-171-6

Stock or custom editions of Ellie Claire titles may be purchased in bulk for educational, business, ministry, fund-raising, or sales promotional use. For information, please e-mail info@EllieClaire.com

Compiled by Rachel Overton
Cover art by istock.com
Cover and interior design by Melissa Reagan
Printed in China

2 3 4 5 6 7 8 9 10 RRD 22 21 20 19 18